THE FACTS ON
PSYCHIC
READINGS

John Ankerberg
& John Weldon

HARVEST HOUSE PUBLISHERS
Eugene, Oregon 97402

Other books by
John Ankerberg & John Weldon

THE FACTS ON PSYCHIC READINGS

Copyright © 1997 by The John Ankerberg Show
Published by Harvest House Publishers
Eugene, Oregon 97402

ISBN 1–56507–560–9

CONTENTS

Preface

Section I
The Psychic Revolution

Section II
A Historical and Scientific Analysis

Section III
A Theological Analysis

Section IV
Psychic Powers: Natural, Supernatural, or Parapsychological?

Section V
Conclusion

3

Preface

Psychics are big news these days. There are numerous 800 or 900 number psychic phone lines. Psychic fairs draw thousands of people in large metropolitan cities across the United States. Police departments use more and more psychics in criminal investigations. Books about the psychic world are regularly on the best-seller lists.[1] And there are now thousands, if not millions, of psychic astrologers, channelers, and diviners, who claim they can tell us the truth about our futures and how to live happy, healthy, successful lives. Even the U.S. government has been seriously involved in psychic research (See question 5).

Recently the public has become much more aware of psychics through TV infomercials such as the Psychic Friends Network (PFN). "Sixty Minutes" correctly described it as "the godzilla of infomercials." PFN is the brainchild of Michael Warren Lasky, the president and CEO of Inphomation Communications who sensed the marketing potential when his company was handling a direct-mail campaign for a New Age magazine. Seeing the phenomenal response to the magazine, he directed his attention to television. And, indeed, the success of these infomercials indicates the extent to which America is now turning to psychics.

Consider a few facts. PFN was named the top infomercial of the year by the Jordon-Whitney "Greensheet," a tracker of the infomercial industry. Since its start up in 1992, every single week that PFN has been on the air, it has grossed at least $1.5 million. (That's a cool $300 million so far.) In 1995, PFN received its 10-millionth phone call. According to co-founder Linda Georgian, president of "Psychics, Inc." and "Linda Georgian TV and Promotions, Inc.," (both are multimedia, multi-marketing TV production corporations) and author of *Communication with the Dead,* "We have the most successful, highest grossing infomercial in the world." In May of 1996, PFN also launched the Psychics Friends Live Radio, a two-hour nationwide program that airs five nights a week. Thus, it's hardly surprising that Jack Schember, publisher of "Response TV" magazine declares that PFN "is not just the most successful psychic infomercial, but literally, the most successful infomercial of all time."[2]

In addition, given the ability of a famous name to make money these days, it's also not surprising that celebrities of all stripes have jumped on the psychic bandwagon. Dionne Warwick, the famous pop singer who, according to Linda Georgian, is also a psychic,[3] heads up the PFN infomer-

4

cials. At one of the rival infomercials, Psychic Readers Network, we find "Miami Vice" co-star Philip Michael Thomas and actor Billy Dee Williams. (The Psychic Readers Network actually boasted "40 million calls last year" on its August 1996 TV ads.) At "The Psychic Solution" we have Nichelle Nichols who played Lt. Uhuru on the original Star Trek TV series—and on it goes. Stars of Hollywood, the music industry and the business world now regularly turn to psychic readings for advice. For example, Linda Georgian recently gave a psychic reading for none other than Donald Trump and stars of "The Young and the Restless." Other stars from popular soaps appear on PFN ads extolling the virtues of psychic readings.[4]

So why are literally millions of people calling psychic hotlines? The reasons are fundamentally practical—to find information about love and relationships, job and career, health and family concerns. Women especially seem to be targets. According to Linda Georgian, the typical caller is a woman in her 30s or 40s.[5] An article in the *Washington Times* reveals, "Those in the know say Psychic Friends mania . . . can be summed up in one word—women. They're the target, and they have been located."[6] Indeed, all one needs to do is examine the leading women's magazines. The end section in *Cosmopolitan* lists all kinds of ads for psychic infomercials, urging women to get the latest information on their love life, careers and financial futures.

At $3.95 a minute, it's easy to see how the bucks come hard and fast for promoters. A simple phone call to a psychic astrologer, dream interpreter or past-life reader for just half an hour, will cost the trusting client $120. And who can deny that it will take time to sort out the complexities of a client's life—not to mention the complexities of a client's future? One assumes that to secure such valuable information, it would be relatively easy for concerned people to pay the going price of $240 an hour.

Of course, at those rates, we also think that predicting a client's financial future is easy.

Section I
The Psychic Revolution

1. What is a psychic and what are psychic readings?

Put simply, a psychic is a person who uses occult, supernatural abilities for a variety of purposes. A psychic reading is the use of an individual's psychic abilities to supply occult information to oneself or a client. The *Oxford American Dictionary* supplies the adjective definition of "psychic" as "concerned with processes that seem to be outside physical or natural laws, having or involving extrasensory perception or occult powers." Psychic as a noun is defined as "a person apparently susceptible to psychic influence, a medium."[7] The *Macmillan Dictionary for Students* defines a psychic as "one who is sensitive to extrasensory, non-physical or supernatural influences or forces."[8]

Professional medium Litany Burns, author of *Develop Your Psychic Abilities,* and "an accredited teacher of psychic awareness in the New York State public school system" defines a psychic reading as "the ability to receive vibrations of energy from another person, place, or living thing and translate it into words or thoughts. . . . You are reading their energy and not their momentary thoughts. Psychic energy, unlike mental energy, is not confined to the physical moment, but encompasses elements of the person's past, present, or future. Fortune telling is a common term for psychic reading . . . your focus is relegated more toward future possibilities than past or present situations."[9]

In other words, a psychic is someone fundamentally connected to the supernatural world of the occult and psychic readings are connected to some method of divination.

Although many people today define the term psychic in its psychological sense, "of the soul or mind" and interpret psychic abilities as a natural potential within all people, we will show why we think it is best to reject this approach. We believe the genuine psychics and psychic readings deal more in the realm of the supernatural and the miraculous, not the natural and the psychological.

2. Why are psychics and psychic readings so popular?

There are many reasons for the modern revival of interest in the psychic realm. In our documentation of the dangers of psychic practices, *The Coming Darkness* (Harvest House, 1993), we discussed a number of them, including 1) the failure of rationalism, secular humanism, and materialism as comprehensive world views; 2) a spiritual vacuum resulting from the cultural abandonment of Christian beliefs and values; 3) the explosive growth of new religions and cults; 4) the influence of rationalistic, liberal theology which rejects the supernatural, thus denying the human need for transcendence; 5) a new parapsychological/New Age view of human potential and the reclassification of psychic powers as something natural and normal, hence legitimate; 6) the freedom from conventional morality offered by the psychic world view and 7) the fact that there is a genuine supernatural world that may be contacted which provides one with power and knowledge normally unavailable.

Also, people are uncertain, even frightened, concerning their future. The relativism and insecurity of the post-Christian age leads people to seek security and absolutes in the realm of the psychic, where supposedly, authoritative answers to life's problems can be found. Unfortunately, the psychic realm is probably the most insecure and risky place one can look to for answers and meaning in life.

But another reason the psychic realm is popular today is that many people are interested in becoming psychics themselves. As internationally acclaimed photographer and psychic, Loretta Washburn, comments, "In the '80s, people wanted the service of psychics, mediums, astrologers and so on. Now, in the '90s, people want to learn to do these things for themselves."[10]

3. Aren't psychic hotlines just cleverly marketed schemes to get people's money?

Many people think the psychic hotlines are simply a con job—savvy promoters hiring minimum wage telemarketers to falsely claim they are psychics to take advantage of the gullible. And this is frequently true. When the Psychic Friends Network first began, although it claimed that clients would be contacting genuine psychics, this was not necessarily the case. Some people were hired who were not psychic.[11]

The truth is that there are many entrepreneurs today who recognize that a bonanza can be made in the "psychic counseling" field. And they are more than willing to give people what they want.

One publication from multi-millionaire Brad Richdale's nationally televised infomercials telling people how to make money supplies the following information about psychic hotlines. It's listed as number 56 of the top 100 products that can be successfully marketed by entrepreneurs:

"Talk to live, true psychics. Explore your romantic future. NOTE: Most 900 service bureaus will provide you with psychics. You can advertise this service and make between $1.50 to $2.50 per minute. Typically, a phone call will take 15 to 30 minutes. But what's even better, people will continue to call their psychics on a regular basis. They develop a relationship and typically will call two or three times a month. You may be skeptical, but there is a large market that isn't. Open up a *National Inquirer* or any other tabloid magazine—the largest classified segment you will see is for psychics and astrology. For over a year and a half, the top infomercial on television has been Dionne Warwick's Psychic Friends. I have several friends who are making fortunes from this business. They have celebrities like Paula Abdul and Randy Travis that call their lines on a regular basis. They do recommend that you research the company that is providing the psychic. The better ones will route the phone calls directly to the psychics' homes. The worst ones will have minimum wage telemarketers read Tarot cards off a computer."[12]

Nevertheless, while psychic infomercials provide the standard disclaimer that their service is "for entertainment purposes only," no one should fail to recognize that PFN and, apparently, most the other major infomercials do seek to hire genuine psychics for their hotlines. Because psychics are so plentiful today, there is little reason to employ frauds. Robert Hoffman, the senior vice-president for Inphomation claims that the psychics on PFN are carefully selected and extensively screened by other psychics so that 80 percent of the applicants are rejected.[13] Peter Stolz, a PRN manager says, "the people who work on the hotline must try to do their divinations by some supernatural means, be it astrology, Tarot cards, or raw psychic power."[14] Further, that real psychics are, in fact, frequently spiritists, is illustrated by Kenna Akash, a trance channeler who channels the spirit "Rojdnan." "Kenna used to work with The Psychic Friends Network, the one you see on television with Dionne Warwick. She gave psychic readings for them, and she now does psychic readings for her own phone line. She has always given personal readings in person or by telephone, with her readings being influenced by Rojdnan."[15]

Of course, none of this is proof that the average caller to a given hotline will get a real psychic or that their psychic powers will be operating successfully at the time of the call; the truth is that psychic powers aren't that reliable.

Regardless, the psychic revolution is here to stay. As *Skeptical Inquirer* noted, "Because of their popularity and profitability, the psychic hotlines are likely to be with us for a long time."[16]

If the psychics are going to be with us for a long time, and, if as they claim, they really are seeking to tap into a supernatural source of information, then what is that source? It would seem to be incumbent upon those who call psychic hotlines, to be certain of the exact nature of the supernatural source that gives them advice on important aspects of their lives. If that source of information is the spirit world, then the implications are hardly insignificant, as we will seek to show. But even if the advice comes only from the psychics themselves, there is no denying it will be colored by the psychic's particular world view—which regardless is characteristically the same as that of the spirits.

Lest Christians think this is an area they need not concern themselves with, perhaps they should listen to Roger E. Olson, associate professor of theology at Bethel College, Saint Paul, Minnesota who observed, "In speaking to church audiences, I have discovered a surprising openness to New Age ideas and practices among middle-age, middle-class Christians."[17] To illustrate, Gallup, Roper and other polls reveal a widespread belief in the world of the psychic generally, including among a surprising number of those who identify themselves as evangelical Christians.

A Gallup poll conducted June 14-17, 1990, showed the belief in the paranormal was "widespread" in American society. This poll also revealed these beliefs are almost as common among those who are "deeply religious in a traditional sense" as among those who are not—even though such beliefs contradict the beliefs of the more traditional religions. Fully 25 percent of Americans believe in ghosts and astrology, one in five believes in reincarnation, including over 20 percent of those who identify themselves as born-again Christians. One in ten Americans believes in channeling and, only 7 percent of Americans denied "believing in of a list of 18 paranormal experiences," including UFOs, psychic healing, contact with the dead, witchcraft and channeling. Almost 50 percent said they believe in five or more of these items and fully 75 percent claimed to have had a personal experience in at least one of these categories.[18]

Another poll revealed that over 40 percent of American adults claimed to have been in contact with someone who died; of these, 78 percent claim they saw, 50 percent heard and 18 percent talked with the dead.[19] Yet another poll indicated 10 percent of "born again" Christians believe in astrology.[20] One could wonder if these poll results are correct, could all this be a fulfillment of the prophecy in 1 Timothy 4:1: "The Spirit clearly says that in later times some will abandon the faith and follow deceiving spirits and things taught by demons (NIV)?"

Regardless, it seems that no one can afford to be ignorant of this subject. Because of its influence, sooner or later, in one way or another, the psychic and psychic reading revival will probably affect all of us.

4. What can psychics do that makes them different from the rest of us?

Although many, and perhaps most, psychics would claim there is no ultimate difference between a psychic individual and one who is not psychic, this is simply not so. Psychics may make this claim only because they believe everyone has the ability to develop the same powers they have, powers that are residing latent in the mind.

The truth is that all people do not have the ability to tap into *latent, natural* psychic powers because such *latent, natural* powers do not exist. What psychics tap into is the one or more spirit-guides who proceed to work through them in an unknown manner for their own purposes. However interfaced with or mediated through the human organism, genuine psychics with supernatural abilities derive their power and knowledge from this source. To illustrate, Enid Hoffman is a psychic and medium and author of *Develop Your Psychic Skill*. On the one hand, she declares that "your psychic abilities are as 'normal' as your physical eyesight and hearing."[21] But then she proceeds to describe how she developed her own psychic abilities through séances.

At one séance a Reverend Raymond Burns was possessed by a spirit. "For nearly two hours voices of different spirit teachers addressed their individual students through Reverend Burns. A new teacher introduced himself to me and my husband, greeting us and warmly welcoming us to the series of séances we would attend to develop our psychic abilities. . . . Gradually, week by week, we became better able to receive ideas telepathically from our [spirit] teachers. . . . With each class our skills improved. Gradually my guesses turned into accurate responses. I didn't really notice the point at which I became convinced at last of the reality of unseen spirits and psychic phenomena. . . . [But]

I became able to give psychic readings and to recall past lives."[22]

In other words, it was only through attending séances and being influenced by spirit-teachers that psychic powers were developed in the first place. We can hardly conclude that such powers are natural human abilities. This is not to say, however, that most psychics develop their powers specifically at séances where the purpose is to directly contact spirits. Psychic powers are often developed in more "neutral" contexts, using only various occult methods or implements such as meditation, altered states of consciousness or tarot cards. In such cases, the power source is not usually recognized as a spirit entity because the spirits often remain behind the scenes. (See pages 40-41 and our chapter on divination in *Encyclopedia of New Age Beliefs* for examples.)

Initially, would-be psychics may only contact what seems to be some impersonal source of energy or power having no discernible location or source. As they maintain a relationship with this power, sooner or later, they find that they are able, more or less "regularly," to do things that normal people cannot do. These include such things as telepathy, clairvoyance, precognition, psychokinesis, out of the body travel, channeling and remote viewing.

Average people simply cannot do such things. Telepathy involves the ability to read minds or transmit thoughts to others. How many people can read the mind of a stranger or transmit their thoughts to someone else?

Clairvoyance is the ability to see events or objects beyond the range of physical vision. How many people can view the events happening at home while they are still at the office?

Precognition is the ability to perceive events in the future. Who can predict the events of tomorrow, let alone events years from now? No one has such an ability unless he or she is aided by some supernatural power outside time and space.

Psychokinesis is the ability to move objects without touching them. How many of us can just sit down and decide we are going to rearrange the objects on a coffee table?

Out of the body experiences involve the alleged ability to detach one's spirit from the physical body and to travel in the spiritual world. Who can logically argue this ability is something common to the human race?

Channeling involves the surrendering of one's mind and body to a spirit entity who then uses it for its own purposes. But anyone familiar with channeling knows that the knowledge derived at this point certainly does not come from the psychic's own mind.[23]

Remote viewing, a form of clairvoyance, is the ability to psychically see events and people at great distances, anywhere on earth; and some claim, even into the past or future. According to a program on the Discovery Channel, noted psychic Ingo Swann could accurately describe a location anywhere on earth just by being given its latitudinal/longitudinal coordinates.[24] How normal is such an ability?

In addition there are other psychic abilities incuding retrocognition, the occult awareness of past events, and psychometry, the ability to sense the past history of an object merely by touching it. Certainly, whatever else one may say about such abilities, they are anything but normal or natural.

In developing psychic abilities, psychics frequently make use of some form of assistance or contact material that somehow helps initiate communication with the spirit world. This includes things like crystals or crystal balls, astrology charts, numerology, séances, Ouija boards, palmistry, pendulums, tarot cards, automatic writing, occult dream interpretation, altered states of consciousness, and occult or Eastern forms of meditation. Today, throughout America, thousands of courses are now offered in psychic development which make use of these and many other methods in order to train people to become psychic.

In conclusion, psychics are not the same as the rest of us, because they often do things that can only be done through spiritistic contact, whether or not such contact is initially evident. Psychics are different in the occult methods they use to develop their abilities, in the occult power source they seek to tap into, and the resulting occult powers they possess.

However, this is not to say that normal people can never have an experience that could be labeled psychic. In rare cases, some people do have such an experience. But this is hardly proof that psychic abilities per se are latent to the human race. Further, we do not believe people should be concerned that such an experience is necessarily evil or spiritistic. In question 15, we have attempted to address this issue in more detail.

5. How involved is the U.S. military in psychic research and application?

Recent news programs and TV specials, as well as official confirmation by the U.S. government, indicate that the

American military has been deliberately involved in the investigation and application of psychic abilities for over two decades. In part, this was a response to serious Soviet investigation into occult powers and abilities for military application. Soviet interests over the years have included work on telepathic hypnosis, how to induce death psychically, psychokinetic applications and much more.[25]

According to one TV program, U.S. military officials stated that in the American research, there had been "a number of remarkable successes over the years." Essentially, for some 25 years, Congress has funded CIA/Pentagon studies in psychic abilities, such as remote viewing or the alleged ability to psychically see events at a distance. The application of such an ability to espionage is obvious. Powerful psychic Ingo Swann was one of those studied, and it was claimed that he had an 85 percent success rate in remote viewing. Shockingly, the Defense Intelligence Agency actually used possessed mediums and channelers in its research. Even some congressmen were said to have sought out the advice of the spirits speaking through these channelers. Those with psychokinetic powers and crystal gazers were also employed. In fact, the U.S. military has called on psychics for some very major operations, including the gathering of covert information on Iraq and Lybia.[26]

According to another program, Dr. David A. Moorehouse took part in secret army experiments relative to remote viewing. It was a vision of an "angel"[27] who told him to stop what he was currently doing in the military and to "seek peace" that got him into the secret psychic experiments headed by the CIA. When he finally left the experiments, he claimed, in all seriousness, the CIA had attempted to kill both him and his family. Today, he deeply regrets his decision to enter the program. It not only ruined his military career, it almost cost him his life and it made his subsequent life extremely difficult. He said, remorsefully, "I just want to be normal again." But he can't because he remains psychic and this places constant strain on him and his family. Although still fascinated by his psychic powers, he confessed, "One of the worst things that happens to remote viewers is that they develop a messiah complex . . . they think they are God." He also points out that even though the CIA claimed to have abandoned its psychic experiments, this was not true. According to Dr. Moorehouse, they never intended to abandon the research, only to take it into a "deep cover status."[28] Even publicly, it was admitted that psychics outside the CIA will continue to be used on a consulting basis.

If all this and more has now been made public, one can only wonder what was private. Or what still goes on? Or what might happen in the future?

Obviously, the implications and consequences for the acceptance of psychic research, occult channeling, etc., at the highest levels of the military, with congressional approval, are extremely serious. If these spirits of the psychics are actually demons, then to have our military seeking the advice of demons is hardly a laughing matter.

Worse still, it is not only through military experimentation that psychics and spiritists gain access to the highest levels of government. We all remember that Nancy Reagan regularly sought the advice of a psychic astrologer, and that such advice affected major decisions by her husband, President Ronald Reagan.[29] Now we discover that Hillary Clinton, the wife of President Bill Clinton, has been seeking the advice of "human potential" expert Jean Houston.[30] What is not so widely publicized is the fact that Houston is also a spiritist. This is documented in her book *Mind Games* as well as her book *The Possible Human,* in which she talks about seeking the advice and help of spirits she calls "master teachers":

"Once you become familiar with your Master Teacher and begin to trust and act on the advice and knowledge that is imparted, you will find it increasingly easy to have access to this kind of deep learning. . . . The Master Teacher is a potent reminder of our inner 'allies' and may often provide much more teaching and wisdom than we had intended when we set off on this journey." Further, "You will evoke a Master Teacher to help you improve this skill [for entering inner realms]. This teacher may be someone you actually know or a major figure from the past such as Leonardo DaVinci, Beethoven, or Einstein, or the persona of the teacher may emerge spontaneously into your consciousness. . . . This teacher will give you deep and potent instructions. . . . The Master Teacher may speak in words or not. Teachings may present themselves as feelings or as muscular sensations. The Master Teacher may have you practice old skills or learn new ones. The teacher may be solemn or quite comical. However this being works with you, the learning on your part will be effective and deep."[31]

Section II
A Historical and Scientific Analysis

6. What can we conclude about psychics when examined and compared historically and today?

Why is it important to look at psychics historically? Because today it is wrongly assumed by many that those with psychic abilities are simply tapping into the "higher powers" of the mind. It is assumed there is nothing supernatural involved with psychics or their abilities since they are only using this "untapped potential." But if we examine psychics historically, we see that psychics are no different from mediums and spiritists generally. Spiritually speaking, they belong to the same family. In other words, in earlier generations, psychics would have been termed mediums, spiritists or even sorcerers. Today, the "difference" between them is largely one of semantics. While it is true that psychics as a whole do not specifically do what séance mediums do (i.e., hold séances to contact the dead), it is nevertheless true that they tap into the same source of power, contact the same spirits, and exhibit the same abilities of mediums and other spiritists.

Anyone knowledgeable about mediums and spiritists knows that these individuals traditionally claim to get their powers and abilities from the spirits they contact. If psychics belong to the same family, then *this* is where we should expect they receive their source of power—not from some nebulous, undemonstrated "human potential." Thus, it is those who argue that psychics should *not* be classed with mediums and spiritists who share the burden of proof: they must offer at least *some* evidence to show that psychics are somehow different from spiritists.

In our next question, we will discover what the discipline of parapsychology can tell us about the nature of psychics and their powers. For now, we will simply document that those who are considered authorities in the psychic realm declare that psychics belong to the category of mediums and spiritists. As we saw, the *Oxford American Dictionary* defined a psychic as "a medium." The authoritative *Encyclopedia of Psychic Science* by noted psychoanalyst and psychic researcher Dr. Nandor Fodor also defines a psychic as, simply, "a medium."[32] In his *The Directory of the Occult*, well-known professor of parapsychology, Hans Holzer declares that "a psychic is a medium."[33]

Even when we turn to the psychics themselves, we can see they are mediums and spiritists. Hope Andrews is the author of *Do Psychics Really Know?*. She was raised as a Christian but became a spiritualist medium, subsequently interpreting her profession through Christian eyes. One of her Indian spirit guides is "Yellow Cloud." There is absolutely no doubt that she is a *medium* yet she calls herself a psychic.[34]

If we look at various books by or about psychics, we find that we are really talking about various classes of mediums and spiritists. In *Mind Travelers: Portraits of Famous Psychics and Healers of Today,* 23 of 29 of the individuals discussed are openly declared to be practitioners of some form of spiritism. In other words, this is a book *about psychics* but it is really a book *about spiritists*. The individuals discussed are Paul Solomon, a trance channeler; Kenna Akash, a trance channeler; Lynn Andrews, a shamaness (a religion characterized by a belief in an unseen world of gods, demons, and ancestral spirits who possess the shaman or shamanes); Sherri Evans Bolling, an astrologer, numerologist and shamaness; "Celeste," an automatic painter; Elaine Eagle Woman, a shamaness; Patricia Hayes, a medium; "Janada," a UFO spiritist; Kathy Lawrance, a spiritist/acupuncturist; William Lawrance ("Wounded Eagle"), a shaman; Jeanie Loomis, a trance channeler; Lin David Martin, a trance channeler; Robin Miller, a trance channeler; Robert Monroe, a spiritist famous for his out of the body travels; Rinatta Paries, an astrologer, energy worker and Reiki practitioner; Foster Perry, a shaman; Sally Perry, a shamaness; Pat Rodegast, a trance channeler; Kevin Ryerson, a trance channeler; Mother Sarita, a psychic surgeon; Sandi Staylor, a spiritist; Judi West, a trance channeler and "Zolar" (Donald Papon), a spiritist, astrologer and homeopath.[35]

Even though Hans Holzer's book is titled *The Directory of Psychics*, it is actually *a directory of mediums*. Holzer himself defines a *"sensitive"* as a "medium" and as a "psychic," and throughout the book the terms "psychic" and "medium" are interchanged.[36] Thus, "Trance mediums are needed, and really fine psychics in this most advanced phase of mediumship are too few. The majority of psychics, readers, interpreters and so forth are clairvoyants, or mental mediums, who perceive their impressions through their minds."[37] And how does one become a psychic? By engaging in methods of mediumistic development.[38] He further states, "Fortunately, practically everybody can develop their psychic abilities to the point of being their own medium."[39]

In *The Psychic Realm: What Can You Believe?,* we again see the influence of spiritism and mediumism through the writing of J. Gaither Pratt, a leading parapsychologist.[40] In a similar fashion there is *An Explosion of Being: An American Family's Journey Into the Psychic* by Douglas and Barbara Dillon. The book title specifically describes a journey into the *psychic realm*. But it is really a journey into *spiritism,* a family's seven-year exploration of mediumism, including specific instructions for contacting the spirit world through dreams, the imagination, and Ouija boards.[41]

Essentially, no matter where we look in the realm of psychics, if there is a single lowest common denominator, it is spiritism. How then did the term "psychic" on the one hand and "medium"/"spiritist" on the other become distanced? Largely it was a result of the discipline of parapsychology, which sought to bring scientific respectability to the study of those with occult powers. By approaching this area scientifically, psychologists had to either downplay the occult and supernatural elements or redefine them as natural and "para" psychological, i.e., as latent but normal powers of the mind. Of course, all this changed nothing concerning the source and nature of the powers themselves; it only changed how they were viewed. As the *Encyclopedia of Occultism and Parapsychology* points out, "Much of the transition from the [mediumistically-based] Psychical Science of the 1900s to the Parapsychology of the last few decades has been largely a *semantic* revolution, riddled with initialisms like ESP and PK as well as statistical analysis of laboratory tests, giving an air of respectability to what was formerly regarded as a very dubious affair of phenomena associated with mediums and Spiritualism."[42]

All this is evidence that "psychics" should really be considered spiritists and mediums, not as a separate class of people with "natural" psychic abilities. In essence, if psychics belong to the same category of individuals as mediums, spiritists and their ancient counterparts, sorcerers and shamans, then we have gone a long way toward properly identifying who we are dealing with when we use the term "psychic." And this is crucial.

7. How does the "scientific" discipline of parapsychology show that psychics and mediums belong in the same category?*

Parapsychology, or psychical research, is the "scientific" study of what is called "psi," a term that refers to psychic events and abilities and/or the energy through which they are accomplished. In modern parapsychology, "psi" is often viewed as either a "new discovery" or as evidence of man's sudden "evolving" to a supposedly higher level—an evolutionary "mutation in consciousness"—allegedly demonstrated through man's ability to perform psychically. Louisa Rhine, wife of the well-known father of modern parapsychology, J. B. Rhine, reflects the scientific, "new discovery" approach when she writes, "One of the most significant advances of science is the discovery that psychic or psi ability is real."[43] David Hammond, author and co-publisher of *Psychic Magazine* (now *New Realities),* reflects the evolutionary view: "What seems clear is that a giant leap forward in human evolution is being taken now. Evolution of the mind, along with the emergence of a psychic sense, has begun."[44]

As noted, parapsychology holds to a basic premise concerning psychic abilities. It assumes that the psychic powers it studies reflect genuinely human potential—latent powers of the mind that anyone can unfold and learn to develop. A standard resource, the *Handbook of Parapsychology*, reflects such a view, referring to psychic powers as "potentialities of the race," "latent human possibility," and "slumbering abilities within the self."[45]

However, even after 130 years of research, the "science" of parapsychology has yet to prove even its most basic premise—that psychic powers represent entirely latent human abilities rather than supernatural powers mediated through individuals, who, knowingly or unknowingly, have come under the influence of spirits.

Nevertheless, the serious scientific research into parapsychology consistently attempts to draw a line between "the occult" on the one hand and "parapsychology" on the other. It apparently does so to convince us that parapsychology is a truly "scientific" field of study and is not involved with the supernatural world of the occult. But this is false.

---

* Excerpted from the author's *Cult Watch*, pp. 272, 276.

Although the methods and sometimes approach of study are different, an examination of the literature in the field, including the publications and research reports of the scientific psi laboratories, clearly show that parapsychologists study occult phenomena and powers. Indeed, for 130 years, mediumism has been the mainstay of parapsychology, even within periods of lessened interest in that particular subject.[46]

Parapsychology was initially founded on the study of spiritistic mediums and its dependence upon those with occult powers remains true today. Parapsychologists are forced to study those persons having occult powers because normal people do not possess such abilities and there is, therefore, nothing to study. That parapsychology is undergirded by mediumism, spiritism, and related practices is confessed by standard texts, such as the *Handbook of Parapsychology*, by leading parapsychologists, such as Gardner Murphy and by the father of parapsychology, J. B. Rhine himself.[47]

Thus, all the major early societies of psychical research were largely engaged in mediumistic/spiritistic investigation or even composed of professed mediums.[48] In 1869, the first serious investigation of spiritism was undertaken by the London Dialectical Society which appointed six subcommittees to investigate mediumship. In the 1870s the Phantasmological Society at Oxford and the Ghost Society at Cambridge also studied mediumism. In 1874, the first public meeting of the British National Association of Spiritualists commenced with most of the prominent spiritists of that time as members. In 1882, with a full two-thirds of its membership comprised of professed mediums, it became what is known today as the famous Society for Psychical Research. In essence, as the late psychical researcher D. Scott Rogo observed, "The major precipitating factor in the development of psychical research was the Spiritualist movement. . . ."[49]

This is why no better definition has ever been proposed of parapsychology, or psychical research, than that put forth by one of the leading psychical authorities of this century, Dr. Nandor Fodor. In his *Encyclopedia of Psychic Science* he defines *psychical* research as "a scientific inquiry into the facts and causes of *mediumistic* phenomena."[50] And, as leading occult authority Colin Wilson points out, "parapsychology is another name for what the ancients called magic."[51]

In conclusion, from its beginning over a century ago until the present, the foundation and sustenance of parapsychological or psychic research has been based upon the study of those with mediumistic or spiritistic powers. We emphasize again that parapsychologists do not profitably study normal people, because normal people are not psychic and there is, therefore, nothing to study. Parapsychologists study those who have occult powers—and such powers are invariably associated with the spirit world.

8. *How accurate are psychic readings and does scientific testing disprove psychic abilities?*

The problem with psychic readings is that they often *aren't* accurate. This is simply a fact. Seeking out psychic readings then, is really a form of metaphysical gambling. There's a small chance you will win but a much larger chance you will lose.

The clients of psychics, like gamblers generally, are optimistic about the possibilities. They want to believe that the positive answers they hear about their future will prove true. However, if people realized that psychics were *mostly* wrong, they would then understand that trusting them is foolish. To get mostly incorrect answers on important areas in life is hardly going to improve one's life.

Indeed, if people actually examined the overall record of psychic predictions, they would never ask a psychic anything. Granting the best *overall* success rate for psychics at 25 percent still leaves us receiving false or bad information 75 percent of the time. The difficulty is that psychics offer more information than just predictions. They may offer commonsense advice, learn to generalize effectively, or offer enough true insights to keep most customers interested. Because psychics deal with people on a regular basis, they learn how to "read" people more effectively and can pick up on clients' moods, concerns, and needs.

Yes, sometimes, psychics can disclose dramatic information about a person that can only be explained supernaturally, and sometimes they can genuinely predict the future. And a small number of psychics have pretty good track records. But this doesn't change the fact of their failures. And even when real psychic abilities are present, this power does not reside in themselves, it comes from their spirit guides. Obviously, their spirit guides don't know everything and further, the spirits have hidden motives for giving such information. One of them is to get clients to accept additional false information on yet more vital topics such as God, Jesus, and salvation.

How do we know that psychics in general are usually wrong when predicting the future?

First, scientific and other experiments have been conducted in a number of different categories testing the abilities of psychics. For example, in our in-depth book on astrology, we examined some of the tests applied to this ancient occult art.[52] Astrologers characteristically get their information psychically, from the spirits, as we also documented in our book, and further, they claim a high success rate. But as we summarized in our *Encyclopedia of New Age Beliefs,* astrologers should never be trusted. One ambitious study examined over 3,000 predictions by leading astrologers including Jeane Dixon, the late Carroll Righter, and witch Sybil Leek, as given in leading astrology publications such as *American Astrology Magazine, Horoscope* magazine, *Astrology* magazine, etc., from 1974 to 1979. The failure rate was almost 90 percent—2,673 of 3,000 predictions were wrong.[cf. 53]

Second, the *Skeptical Inquirer* and related journals regularly test the predictions of leading psychics. For example, every year, the January/February issue of the *Skeptical Inquirer* briefly examines some of the leading psychics' overall track record. In their January/February 1996 issue, the article headlined, "Psychics Missed It Big (Again) in 1995" and they noted such false predictions as Rush Limbaugh being forced to go on welfare, Disney World being wiped out by a hurricane, promises of cures for AIDS, and TV journalist Peter Jennings becoming the first journalist in space.[54]

Third, psychics themselves admit they make mistakes. Psychic Friends Network co-founder, Linda Georgian, confesses, "Nobody's 100 percent accurate. . . . If they claim to be as a psychic, it's a scam."[55] Along with other false predictions, Georgian herself predicted in the January 3, 1995 *National Examiner* tabloid that Beverly Hills' madam Heidi Fleiss would "convert to Catholicism" and become a nun![56]

Thus, if we simply examine the predictions psychics give in print, and wait long enough, we can see that their predictions should never be trusted. For example, Jeane Dixon is one of America's most well-known psychics. In her book, *The Call to Glory,* first published in 1971, she made a number of predictions about the future. Like many psychics, she claims that Jesus has spoken to her personally. Feeling "an overpowering spiritual presence," she claims, "as others, I too have seen Jesus and listened to His voice."[57] But consider a few of her false predictions: "In 1978 the United States will be caught in the throws of a depression brought about by vast social and political giveaways and internal subversion." Obviously, she was wrong. Then she says, "The future has been shown to me to 2037" and proceeds to predict the future in 19-year cycles. From the period 1980-1999 we are told, "This period will be triggered by a natural disaster in the Middle East. An earthquake of major proportions will be the signal advantage for an invasion of Israel by its neighbors. Battles will continue until 1988 . . . the Russians and their satellite armies will move into the area and occupy the lands of all participants. More battles, bloodshed, massacres, misery, and pestilence will continue until 1995. . . . Since the major events will be in the Middle East, our headquarters will be in Rome. In 1995 great allied armies will begin the build up to strike at the Russian forces, apprehensive despite all their success. . . ."[58]

In spite of such obvious false predictions, millions of people continue to trust in Jeane Dixon as "a prophetess of God"! God, however, never makes mistakes. The biblical standard for a true prophet of God is 100 percent accuracy in predictions, period (Deuteronomy 18:22; Jeremiah 28:9). By definition then, anything less than 100 percent makes someone a false prophet. Do we ever find God's prophets hedging their bet, like modern psychics do? Can we imagine the prophet Jeremiah prophesying to Israel, "Thus, saith the Lord, 'I'm pretty sure this is going to happen,—but I can't give you any guarantees'"? But this is exactly what psychics are forced to do because they know their track record is imperfect. In essence, what proves psychics' revelations are not from God is the false predictions: no psychic dead or alive has a perfect record.

But when examining psychics scientifically and critically an important point must be made.

Scientific testing does not disprove the existence of psychics' abilities; it only proves that psychic abilities are characteristically incapable of experimental replication in a scientific laboratory under rigid clinical trials.

The error materialists make when evaluating psychics is to conclude that psychic powers don't exist simply because they cannot be replicated or proven scientifically. Of course there are many things that exist and yet cannot be scientifically replicated in a laboratory setting. No spirit can be proven to exist scientifically yet we know spirits exist from both biblical revelation and the testimony of history. The same is true for psychic powers. Psychics can and do tap into genuine supernatural power that sometimes actually does perform miracles, such as predicting the future or giving startling self-disclosures to their clients—i.e., secret information known only to their clients.

Regardless, those who trust the readings of psychics do so at their peril. Not only are many "psychics" frauds, but even most of the genuine psychics have an overall poor track record. When it is further understood psychics may get their information from deceptive spirits, only the foolish would proceed to trust a psychic. Indeed, there are far too many cases of bad advice that ruined people's relationships, health, finances, etc., simply because people trusted what psychics told them.

Yet despite this poor record, psychics claim that their "gift" comes from God. (One wonders what this does to people's faith in God?) To the contrary, the following section will prove beyond a doubt that psychic readings cannot come from God.

Section III
A Theological Analysis

9. What is the basic theological world view of psychics, and how does it compare with the biblical world view?

As noted, psychics usually claim their abilities come from God and their personal philosophy is in harmony with divine interests. Some even claim their powers come directly from Jesus or that their abilities are the biblical gifts of the Holy Spirit. However, they really don't know where their powers come from; they only assume they are divine. But if we examine their teachings, we can see that the world view of psychics and that of the Bible are opposed to one another at every point. What this means is that psychics cannot logically claim a positive association with God or Jesus, or that their beliefs are compatible with Christian belief when their personal philosophy is so thoroughly anti-biblical.

If the basic world view of psychics can be summed up in a word, we would have to describe it as fundamentally spiritistic. That is, the world view of psychics is essentially that of the spirit world as revealed through channelers, mediums and other spiritists. Psychics universally reject the biblical teaching on creation, man, salvation, death, the afterlife, and morality. While the basic world view of psychics is also in general harmony with that of many other religions, especially Eastern religions, it is definitely opposed to biblical Christianity. What would this imply? This would indicate that the source behind psychic revelations has a bias against biblical teachings.

Let us give you a few examples. In *Ascended Masters Speak to Us Today*, psychic Reverend Beverly Burdick-Carey writes as follows. (Actually, these are the teachings of her various spirit guides given to her in a séance which she accepts as divine truth)[59]: "Quan Yin" declares "GOD is ALL there is!. . . . GOD is ONE, ONE is ALL, ALL is GOD! Each of you is a manifestation of the consciousness of GOD. . . . YOU are GOD in manifestation."

"Saint Germain" gives us the following bit of environmentally friendly and enlightening advice, "GOD IS ALL. GOD IS ULTIMATE HEALING POWER WITHOUT LIMITATIONS . . . [therefore even] the cockroach has healing energy to share with you, and will willingly do so . . . cats, dogs, birds, fish, various rodents such as guinea pigs, [should be your] choice in sharing healing energy and in asking that they help you to heal. . . . When you hug a tree, you merge your chakra system with the chakra system of the tree. The tree will heal you. You will heal the tree."

"Mary" the mother of Jesus tells us, "GOD is ONE, ONE is ALL, ALL is GOD! If you substitute the word LOVE for the word GOD, the equation is still correct. . . . You seek to be EnChristed. You seek to wear the title CHRIST, the Anointed ONE! . . . . You are a precious eternal portion of the consciousness of Soul, the Mind of GOD."[60]

We have prepared the following chart to indicate the basic world view of most psychics to show how this compares and contrasts with biblical Christianity. If, as the evidence dictates, biblical Christianity is a true revelation from God, then the world view based on the revelations given to psychics cannot be.[61]

BIBLICAL CHRISTIANITY	PSYCHIC/NEW AGE

GOD

An infinite personal Father, Son and Holy Spirit (Matt. 28:19; Rom. 15:30; 2 Cor. 13:14).

An infinite impersonal force. God may be considered a universal law, an impersonal principle, universal consciousness or energy, etc.

MAN

Man was created in God's image (Gen. 1:27), and as such is a finite creation who will never become God (Isa. 14:13-15; Isa. 43:10; 44:8; Ezek. 28:1-2, 9; 1 Thess. 4:17).

Man in his true nature is fully one essence with God.

SIN

A willful violation of God's moral law and character (1 Jn. 5:17).

Ignorance of one's personal divinity, and the consequences flowing from this.

JESUS

The only incarnation and Son of God (Jn. 3:16, 18); undiminished deity and full humanity in one person, the unique God-man (cf., Phil. 2:5-9); Col. 2:9; Jesus was born the Christ (Lk. 2:11) and to deny that Jesus was born the Christ is to be "anti-christ" (1 Jn. 4:2-3).

For psychics, Jesus was the greatest psychic of all, the one who proved our divine potential, i.e., that we all can develop psychic abilities like He did in order to grow spiritually and to help others. Jesus is only an example of a man who realized his divine nature and became enlightened; therefore through proper use of knowledge *(gnosis)* the man Jesus *became* the Christ (i.e., enlightened).

SALVATION

Salvation involves forgiveness of sin and justification as a free gift of God's mercy and grace (Rom. 3:23, 5:1,9,15).

Salvation involves "enlightenment" i.e., release from one's ignorance in thinking one is a limited creature and/or individual personality rather than one in nature with the impersonal God. Salvation is earned, not a free gift.

DEATH

There is only one lifetime prior to divine judgment (Heb. 9:27); physical death involves the separation of the spirit from the body; spiritual death involves the eternal separation of the spirit from God (Matthew 25:46).

Death is an "illusion" and carries no final consequences. Through reincarnation, psychic philosophy teaches universalism, that all entities will finally be "saved."

In conclusion, the above chart is proof that, no matter what their claims, the world view of psychics is not biblical. If the Bible is God's revelation to us, then the psychics cannot be getting their revelations from God. Our next question will document this further.

10. What does the Bible say about psychics and psychic readings?

We saw in question 6 that considered historically and logically, psychics really belong in the category of spiritists and mediums. And the Bible has a great deal to say about such individuals. For example, God forbids contact with them, because to do so is something that will spiritually defile or corrupt people by leading them to worship false gods. Spiritism is so evil that capital punishment itself was prescribed in the Old Testament for those who became spiritists and even for those who sought advice from them. In other words, consulting a spiritist was no less sinful than being one.

> Do not turn to mediums or seek out spiritists, for you will be defiled by them. I am the Lord your God (Leviticus 19:31).

> And he . . . [King Manasseh of Judah] practiced witchcraft, used divination, practiced sorcery, and dealt with mediums and spiritists. He did much evil in the sight of the Lord, provoking him to anger (2 Chronicles 33:6 NASB).

> I will set my face against the person who turns to mediums and spiritists to prostitute himself by following them, and I will cut him off from his people. . . . A man or woman who is a medium or spiritist among you must be put to death. You are to stone them; their blood will be on their own heads (Leviticus 20:6, 27).

Further, psychics are also diviners, that is, they seek to divine or predict the future. Biblically, however, diviners fall into the category of false prophets who lead people away from the true God. In other words, according to the Bible, to be a diviner who claims to speak for God is to be a false prophet who leads people away from the true God. The Old Testament penalty for this was also death (Deuteronomy 13:5).

All this shows how serious it is to be a psychic. Here are some other statements in the Bible about diviners and false prophets:

> If a prophet, or one who foretells by dreams, appears among you and announces to you a miraculous sign or wonder, and

if the sign or wonder of which he has spoken takes place, and he says, "Let us follow other gods" (gods you have not known) "and let us worship them," you must not listen to the words of that prophet or dreamer. The Lord your God is testing you to find out whether you love him with all your heart and with all your soul (Deuteronomy 13:1-3).

Let no one be found among you who sacrifices his son or daughter in the fire, who practices divination or sorcery, interprets omens, engages in witchcraft, or casts spells, or who is a medium or spiritist or who consults the dead. . . . The nations you will dispossess listen to those who practice sorcery or divination. But as for you, the Lord your God has not permitted you to do so (Deuteronomy 18:10, 11, 14).

For rebellion is like the sin of divination . . . (1 Samuel 15:23a).

. . . Do not practice divination or sorcery (Leviticus 19:26b).

Then the Lord said to me, "The prophets are prophesying lies in my name. I have not sent them or appointed them or spoken to them. They are prophesying to you false visions, divinations, idolatries and the delusions of their own minds" (Jeremiah 14:14).

One reason God rejects the psychics is because psychics reject God. Actively or passively they lead people away from the one true God and from faith in Jesus Christ. Consider three biblical examples. We read that "Jannes and Jambres opposed Moses" (2 Tim. 3:8, cf., Ex. 7:11ff). Tradition tells us Jannes and Jambres were two of the Egyptian sorcerers (or psychics) that attempted to duplicate Moses' miracles. They did so to prove their powers were as great as Moses, that Moses did not have the one true God on his side and, thus that Pharaoh was not obligated to listen to Moses and release the Israelites from slavery (Ex. 7:11). In the book of Acts we read of a Jewish sorcerer and false prophet named "Bar-Jesus" who "opposed them [Paul and Barnabas] and tried to turn the proconsul [Sergius Paulus] from the faith" (Acts 13:6-8). In Revelation we read of the false prophetess Jezebel who encouraged pagan practices in the church: "By her teaching she misleads my servants into sexual immorality and the eating of food sacrificed to idols." (Revelation 2:20).

We also read that when people rejected the occult, Christianity advanced. "Many of those who believed now came and openly confessed their evil deeds. A number who had practiced sorcery brought their scrolls together and burned them publicly. When they calculated the value of the scrolls, the total came to fifty thousand drachmas. In this way the word of the Lord spread widely and grew in power" (Acts 19:18-20).

In essence, when we read of psychics, occultists, sorcerers, magicians or false prophets in the Bible, we see that directly or indirectly they are seeking to turn people away from the one true God. This is not merely because their world view is anti-biblical; it is because such individuals are characteristically manipulated by spirits who have hidden agendas. In other words, there is a logical reason that the psychics of history and today are so opposed to biblical Christianity. It is because the spirit powers they contact secretly hate it.

In part, all this explains why the Bible's condemnation of psychics is so uncompromising. Going to psychics defiles people. It not only gives people false information that can harm their lives physically or emotionally, it gives them teachings from demons that will harm them spiritually and prevent them from finding salvation. This explains why all the above scriptures condemn psychics: 1) They oppose God and lead people away from Him; 2) they oppose biblical teachings and 3) they lead people to trust in demons (1 Timothy 4:1).

Section IV
Psychic Powers: Natural, Supernatural or Parapsychological?

11. How are psychic powers developed?

Psychic powers are developed in three principal ways: 1) heredity, 2) psychic development and 3) transference.

There is little doubt that psychic powers can be hereditary. We surveyed some of the evidence for this in *The Coming Darkness*[62] and it is discussed by authorities such as Dr. Nandor Fodor, Dr. Kurt Koch, Dr. Merrill Unger and others. As Dr. Fodor states, "In most cases mediumship can be traced as a hereditary gift. If the heredity is not direct it is to be found in ancestors or collaterals."[63] Dr. Koch observes, "In a long series of cases it has been possible to establish that occult subjection is an especially marked psychological constitution lasting through four succeeding generations of the same family."[64]

The compilation by the editors of *Psychic* magazine—*Psychics: Indepth Interviews* reveals a consistent pattern. Most psychics interviewed admitted familial involvement. Famous mediums Arthur Ford, Eileen Garrett, and Douglas

Johnson all had aunts who were mediums or psychics; Irene Hughes and Peter Hurkos had mothers who were psychic and virtually all 19 members of witch Sybil Leek's nuclear and extended family were sympathetic to the psychic realm.[65]

One of America's most successful psychics is Sylvia Brown (her spirit guide is "Francine"). Brown observes, "Being psychic is a family pattern which includes my grandmother Ada Coil, an uncle, and my youngest son Christopher Dufresene. The genetic aspect is important, but it is not the truest measure of what being psychic really entails."[66] Yolana Lassaw is a famous trance medium and clairvoyant in New York. Her son Ron Bard inherited her psychic ability. Hans Holzer comments, "Bard has certainly inherited his mother's considerable psychic gift."[67]

Some wonder how something like a psychic predisposition could be inherited. No one knows. However, if physical things like alcohol, drugs and sexually transmitted diseases can affect an unborn child physically, can we be certain that spiritual sins can never affect a child spiritually? Of course, no one is predestined to become psychic and neither are righteous children punished for the sins of their parents (Deuteronomy 24:16; Ezekiel 18:19-20). However, there clearly is some kind of transmission that often occurs and the means of it are not as important as the fact of it. This is why seeking to become psychic is dangerous. If people will not avoid the psychic realm for their own welfare, they should do it for the sake of their children.

Psychic development is a second means to become psychically active. Classes are now offered throughout America by occultists on how to develop your psychic abilities, tap into your "inner potential" or "higher mind," to release your "hidden powers." There are a hundred different ways to develop psychically from attending séances, to developing altered states of consciousness, self-hypnosis classes, yoga practice, and visualization methods. However, when there is no hereditary transmission, psychic powers developed this way may take months or years to emerge successfully. The point here is that without specific occult instruction and technique, these powers are not developed. If the potential for psychic development is only present to those in the proper "environment" (occultism, proximity to spirits), then there *is* no potential to develop psychically outside that context. Therefore, the potential for psychic development must be considered specific to certain individuals, not universal to the human race. The only exceptions are heredity or transference.

Nor is this anything new. In 1920, the distinguished psychic investigator Dr. Hereward Carrington wrote *Your Psychic Powers and How to Develop Them,* which continues in print today. He observes that the basic method for psychic development is through various methods and practices of mediumship and that this is always the path one must take.

Third, psychic powers may also be transferred from one psychic to a student or understudy. For example, the more powerful Eastern gurus such as Rajaneesh, Muktananda and Sai Baba could transmit occult power that would "open" their disciples to the psychic realm. The transmission of occult power from guru to disciple in initiation (*Shaktipat diksha*) or at other times, can have an extremely dramatic impact on a person's life.

In fact, this dramatic transfer of energy is frequently self-described as an experience of possession.[68] Thus, "If the disciple is really surrendered, the Master can possess him immediately. And once you are possessed by the energy of the Master, once his prana [divine energy] surrounds you, enters you, much is done very easily which you cannot do in years."[69]

One fledgling psychic told us that when her master psychic went into an altered state of consciousness and touched her on the forehead that powerful currents of energy began to enter her head and go down through her body. She could feel parts of her body "opening" and the entire experience was incredibly blissful and pleasant. She was convinced that she had an experience with God. The energy began to move around within her more dramatically, shaking her limbs and various thoughts were being impressed into her mind. That very evening she began to develop psychic abilities.

When Swami Muktananda initiated Albert Rudolph (who was to become Swami Rudrananda), he recalled, "Immediately I felt within me a surge of great spiritual force which hurled me against the stone walls and allowed a great electric shock to send a spasm of contortions through my body. Movements similar to an epileptic fit controlled my body for almost an hour. Many strange visions appeared, and I felt things opening within me that had never been opened before."[70]

There may also be a transference of occult abilities merely from being in the proper environment, irrespective of the intent to become psychic. This may happen through simply being a sitter at a séance or having certain physical contact with the person possessing occult abilities. Water dowsing is an example.[71] The authority on occult counseling, the late Dr. Kurt Koch writes, "Another way of receiving mediumistic abilities is through occult transference. If someone with the ability to use a [dowsing] rod or pendulum holds the hands of a person without the ability, a transference can take place which surprisingly is permanent. Transferred powers, however, are never as strong as inherited ones."[72] As two life-long magical practitioners point out, "Many people who, from one cause or another, had real difficulty in finding and developing their dowsing ability, have experienced a complete change in the situation when they were helped by an established dowser, who placed his or her hands upon their arms while they held the fork. . . . Dowsing is one of the most readily 'contagious' of psychic powers. . . ."[73]

Dr. Nandor Fodor observes, "The spread of modern spiritualism discloses the phenomenon of mediumistic induction. Those who sat with the Fox sisters usually discovered mediumistic abilities in themselves. . . . The most famous early [psychic] investigators became mediums. Judge Edmonds, Professor Hare, William Howitt [all] confessed to have received the gift. . . . H. Dennis Bradley received the power of direct voice [mediumship] after his sittings with George Valiantine. The marquis Centurione Scotto developed through the same instrumentality. Eusapia Paladino could transfer her powers by holding the sitter's hand."[74]

In conclusion, psychic abilities are not from God; they are not divine gifts and they should never be confused with the gifts of the Holy Spirit mentioned in the Bible.[75] Psychic abilities are spiritistic powers invariably associated with occultists and occult practices.

12. Does the Bible imply that psychic abilities are innate potentials of the human race?*

It is our conviction that not only the history of the psychic and the occult, but biblical teaching as well, indicate that human nature is devoid of the supernatural capacities that psychics and occultists claim. Nowhere in the Bible is man presented as having supernatural powers that originate from his own nature. Any truly supernatural miracles performed by men or women must originate either from a divine or a demonic source—either from God and the good angels or Satan and the fallen angels (demons).

---

* Exerpted from the authors' *Cult Watch* p. 268, q. 10.

This is why when we examine the Bible, we discover that the miracles done by believers are done entirely through the power of God, or holy angels.*

Which biblical prophet was able to do miracles apart from God's power? Who were the disciples before Jesus gave them authority? Did any of them perform miracles? Even the greatest, most godly man alive, apart from Jesus, never did a single miracle (John the Baptist, Matthew 11:11; John 10:41). Likewise, the most dramatic miracle performer, apart from Jesus, was Moses. But Moses confessed that his power to perform miracles was not his own, but God's alone (Exodus 3:11, 20; 4:1-17). Jesus Himself taught, "Apart from me you can do nothing" (John 15:5).

Further, note the thrust of the following Scriptures. Collectively, they strongly imply that there is no latent psychic ability for men and women to develop.

In Acts 16:16-19 we find the story of the slave girl who had "a spirit of divination." Significantly, when the Apostle Paul cast the spirit out of the girl, she lost her psychic powers. "And it [the spirit] came out at that very moment. But when her masters saw that their hope of profit was gone, they seized Paul and Silas and dragged them into the market place before the authorities." Now if this girl's powers were innate and natural, why did she lose them the very moment that the spirit was cast out of her? It would seem evident that the psychic powers came from the spirit, not the girl. For those who hold to biblical authority, this single episode speaks volumes about the mushrooming claims in our day to allegedly natural, neutral energies or powers that can be developed by anyone.

Moses, the greatest prophet in the Old Testament, had no power except from God. As noted, Moses openly confessed the miracles he performed were not from his own hand. God Himself spoke specifically to Moses: "So I will stretch out My hand, and strike Egypt with all *My miracles* which I shall do in the midst of it" (Exodus 3:20, cf. Deuteronomy 34:11-12 NASB). "See that you perform before Pharaoh all the wonders *which I have put* in your power" (Exodus 4:21 Emphasis added).

What was true for Moses has been consistently true for every other Old Testament biblical prophet who performed miracles: Elijah, Elisha, Daniel. Their power came from the "Spirit of the Lord" (cf. Micah 3:8).

---

* Even in the category of spiritual gifts, the nature of a gift implies a person does not possess it prior to its being given.

In the New Testament we find the same situation—apart from God the apostles had no power on their own. The apostles were "clothed with power from on high" by God, the Holy Spirit (Luke 24:49; Acts 2:4, 43). For example, in the healing of the lame beggar in Acts 3:12, NASB "When Peter saw this [the people's amazement over the miraculous healing], he replied to the people, 'Men of Israel, why do you marvel at this, or why do you gaze at us, as if by our own *power or piety* we had made him walk?'" (Emphasis added).

The Apostle Paul and Barnabas reflected the same attitude. In Acts 14:11-15 we find the crowd that had witnessed their miracles attempting to worship Barnabas and Paul: "And when the multitudes saw what Paul had done, [they said]. . . . 'The gods have become like men and have come down to us. . . .' [but Paul said] "Men, why are you doing these things? We are also men of the *same nature* as you. . . ." In Acts 10:26 Cornelius attempted to worship Peter after seeing his miracles, but Peter responded, "Stand up; I too am *just* a man." In Acts 4:29-30, NIV Peter prayed, "Now, Lord. . . . Stretch out *your hand* to heal and perform miraculous signs and wonders. . . ." In Acts 14:3, "Therefore they spent a long time there speaking boldly with reliance upon the Lord, who was bearing witness to the word of His grace, *granting* that signs and wonders be done by their hands." In Acts 9:34, "And Peter said to him, 'Aeneas, *Jesus Christ* heals you. . . .'" In Acts 19:11, "And *God* was performing extraordinary miracles by the hands of Paul." In Romans 15:19, ". . . in the power of signs and wonders, in the *power of the Spirit;* . . . I have fully preached the gospel of Christ." Jesus himself said in Luke 10:19, "Behold, *I have* given you authority . . . and over all the power of the enemy. . . ." Further, in James 5:17: "Elijah was a man with a *nature like ours,*" and he *"prayed earnestly"*—only then a miracle from God resulted. (Emphasis added in the above verses. All quotes in this section from the NASB unless noted.)

Similar verses declaring that divine miracles come from God and not from man are found in Genesis 41:16, Daniel 1:17, 20; 2:27-30, Mark 6:7, Acts 15:12, 16:17, 19:11, Romans 15:19, 1 Corinthians 12:9, 10, 28, 30.

But if the Bible teaches that men have no supernatural powers, it is just as clear that the devil does have them and that he can perform true miracles (e.g., 2 Thessalonians 2:9).

The evidence, then, would seem clear. Occultists themselves frequently admit they have no psychic abilities apart form their spirit guides. The Bible also testifies that men are without latent supernatural power and that miracles come from one of two sources: God or Satan. Finally, over a century of intensive parapsychological study has failed to produce any genuine evidence of latent psychic ability. Even after 130 years of serious research into the psychic realm, we not only do not know the nature of psi but there is no scientific evidence that it even exists as a human ability. In his historical overview of parapsychology, noted parapsychologist John Beloff comments, "When it comes to the basic nature of psi, we are still almost as much in the dark as were our pioneers. Theories and models in plenty have been put forward, but they are little more than speculative exercises which so far lack empirical support. . . ."[76]

Consider the comments of Danny Korem, a world-class stage magician who has investigated or exposed a number of leading psychics. Responding to the question, "Do humans actually possess psychic powers?" he replied: "If you mean by psychic abilities things the mind can do in and of its own ability, I say it's not possible. That's what you find when you investigate case after case after case. Tens of millions of dollars have been spent on research in this area and there has never been a verifiable demonstration of human psychic power."[77]

All of this indicates that man is not the psychic and supernatural creature that many in the New Age and the modern revival of the occult claim he is.

13. What have psychics themselves stated about their abilities?*

If those who claim psychic powers (and acknowledge the presence of spirits in their lives) freely confess that apart from their spirit guides, they have no supernatural abilities, then where do those who do not acknowledge the presence of spirits get their powers from? Psychics, diviners, shamans, satanists, witches, mediums, channelers, psychic healers and spiritists of every stripe freely concede, that apart from their spirit helpers, they are powerless to do the things that they do.

Michael Harner has been a visiting professor at Columbia and Yale. He teaches anthropology courses in the graduate faculty of the New School for Social Research in New York and is chairman of the Anthropology section of the New York Academy of Sciences. He is also a practicing shaman and author of *The Way of the Shaman*. He observes that the fundamental source of power for all shamans is the spirit

---

* Part of the following is excerpted from *Cult Watch*, pp. 257-60.

world: "Whatever it is called, it is the fundamental source of power for the shaman's functioning. . . . Without a guardian spirit, it is virtually impossible to be a shaman, for the shaman must have this strong, basic power source . . ."[78]

Concerning Hindu and Buddhist gurus, which incidentally, have many characteristics in common with the shaman,[79] they, too, confess that their power comes from the spirit world. No less an authority than Indies Shah observes, "It is true that the Sadhus [gurus] claim that their power comes exclusively from spirits; that they within themselves possess no special abilities except that of concentration."[80]

Louis Jacolliot, a former Chief Justice of the French East Indies and Tahiti confesses the same. In *Occult Science in India and Among the Ancients,* he observes that psychic forces are conceded to be "under the direction of the spirits."[81] Thus, the Indian psychics "produce at will the strangest phenomena entirely contrary to what are conventionally called natural laws. With the aid of spirits who are present at all their operations, as claimed by the Brahmans, they have the authority as well as the power, to evoke them."[82]

In his *Adventures into the Psychic,* seasoned psychic researcher Jess Stearn makes the common observation that, "Almost without exception, the great mediums . . . felt they were instruments of a higher power which flowed through them. They did not presume to have the power themselves."[83]

In other words, people who have this power characteristically recognize it is *not* a natural human ability. In *Freed from Witchcraft,* former Satanist and witch Doreen Irvine confesses, "I had known and felt that [occult] power often enough, but I believed it was not a natural, but rather a supernatural, power working through me. I was not born with it. The power was not my own but Satan's."[84] Significantly, even as a Satanist and witch she *did not know* that she was possessed by numerous demons; "Now, I was no stranger to demons. Had I not often called on them to assist me in rites as witch and Satanist? [But now] For the first time I knew these demons were within me, not outside. It was a startling revelation."[85]

Apparently then, even the most demonized individuals such as Irvine, who had 47 demons cast from her,[86] need not be consciously aware that spirits are indwelling them. If so, it may be logical to assume that many others who traffic in less virulent forms of the occult may also be influenced possessed by demons and yet not know it.

Further, if such people are cleverly taught that their supernatural powers are "natural and innate," they will wrongly assume that their powers originate within them as some "natural" or evolutionary psychic ability. The fact that demons work through them would not only be hidden from them, there would be a natural aversion to the very concept of demons because the concept of "natural powers" is infinitely preferable to the idea of collusion with evil, supernatural spirits. This is one premise of much occultism; that nothing is truly supernatural. In the end, everything is a "natural" part of the "creation." As one occult manual observes, "We will adopt the view that there is no such thing as the supernatural: whatever exists must be natural . . ."[87] Even some mediums view their quite real spirit-guides as parts of their own unconscious minds. As famous trance medium Eileen J. Garrett wrote in her autobiography, "I long ago accepted them as working symbols of the subconscious . . . a fact which is known to them and troubles them not at all."[88]

Nevertheless, however occultists may choose to interpret their powers, they cannot escape the fact that it really is spirits that work through them. For example, consider the phenomenon of psychic healing which many people consider a "natural" and/or "divine" ability. In his *Supersenses*, Charles Panati refers to the research of psychic researcher Lawrence LeShan who has observed Eastern and Western psychic healers first hand. Panati states, "But if the healers he studied had one thing in common, it was that they all felt that they did not perform the healing themselves; 'a "spirit" did it working through them.' They felt they were merely passive agents. . . . All the healers he studied slipped into altered states of consciousness in order to heal."[89]

One of the most comprehensive collections of information on psychic healing is *Healers and the Healing Process*. This authoritative 10-year investigation observes, "Any study of healers immediately brings the investigator face to face with the concept that spirit intelligences (variously referred to as guides, controls, or protectors) are working through the minds of healers to supply information of which the healer himself has no conscious knowledge."[90]

This study also noted that, "the only large concentrations of healers seemed to be in countries where the belief systems involve what is generally known as spiritualism or spiritism."[91] For example, "In both Brazil and the Philippines the healers have developed almost entirely in the confines of spiritualistic communities."[92]

Even psychics themselves and psychic researchers will sometimes confess that psychic abilities are *not* natural or latent but are actually rare and supernatural. Noted psychic Douglas Johnson comments, "Many people seem to think that everybody's psychic. I personally don't believe that.... [Those with] true psychic ability ... are very few."[93]

Professor George Henslow of Christ College, Cambridge and later president of the British Association for the Advancement of Science decided to use a pen name on a book he wrote called *Spirit-Psychometry*. Professor Henslow concludes that psychometric "visions and impressions are largely, if not wholly, imparted to the seer by unseen agencies" ie., spirits.[94] Occult authority Colin Wilson comments on this book:

> Henslow concluded *Spirit-Psychometry* with a chapter in which he summarizes the evidence. He is of the opinion that psychometry is probably a form of mediumship, and that it is spirits who communicate various impressions to the psychometrist.... *Spirit-Psychometry* is a work of central importance in the history of psychometry ... the part of this book dealing with spiritualism is also impressive and convincing. ... Psychometry and clairvoyance and precognition and mediumship *tend to overlap*. Once we accept any one of them, it is almost impossible not to be drawn into accepting most of the others.... Henslow is willing to submit highly convincing evidence for the reality of spirits and their connection with psychometry....[95]

This admission is important. In the literature of psychic research, psychometry is often held up as an example of an entirely natural psychic ability. If the evidence is so persuasive for psychometry being spiritistic, then on what basis can we argue that psychic abilities generally are natural or psychological and not spiritistic?

Indeed, if we read widely enough in the psychic and spiritistic literature, we discover that the spirits themselves will admit that *they* are the ones that give psychic abilities to people, including everything from altered states to out of the body travels, psychokinesis, telepathy, etc. We give many examples in our *Encyclopedia of New Age Beliefs*.[96] Here are more examples. In *Develop Your Psychic Abilities*, Litany Burns, a professional medium declares that "[spirit] *Guides* can help you develop your psychic and creative abilities, adding their energy to your own *spirit's* energy...."[97] She says that spirit guides can help people develop their clairvoyant and psychokinetic powers: "Your *guide* can help you develop your own *clairvoyant* ability when working with your *spirit,* your *guide* can assist your *spirit* by sharing its own perceptions and helping to transfer them to your body" and "when using any psychic ability your *guides,* body, and *spirit* can help you focus your energies. . . . Your *guide* can use its own energy to help you move or lift a physical object."[98]

This immediately raises a question: If the spirits' assistance is necessary to help people become psychic, can people become psychic apart from the spirits' assistance? In essence, psychics are an integral *component* of spiritism, not separate from it. There are not two groups—psychics who deal only with natural, human psychic powers and spiritists who deal only with supernatural powers. Indeed, the relationship between psychics and spirits/mediums is so close that our book on channeling, *The Facts on Spirit-Guides* could almost have easily been titled, *The Facts on Psychics*. After all what psychic ability, power or event exists that cannot be accomplished by the spirits?

Section V
Conclusion

14. What are some personal and national consequences of the psychic revolution?

While the life of a psychic can be interesting, it is also often miserable. To illustrate, the following comments by psychic Sylvia Brown could sooner or later apply to just about any psychic: "Psychics are really just human beings with a gift, [a gift] which does not serve us personally very well. . . . My life reads like a struggle for survival. . . . Someone told me that I am a 'karmic catharsis' for everyone, which seems to fit well."[99] As is usually true, psychics' spirit guides warn them in advance that their lives will be difficult and perilous. Apparently, what few psychics have considered is that because of their basic philosophy of life, which includes ideas such as karma, their spirit guides are free to induce all the suffering and misery they wish, explaining this as a necessary consequence of the psychics' need for karmic "readjustment" from misdeeds in "past lives."*

---

* Of course, if being a psychic in this life means one is so spiritually advanced, how could the karmic debt weigh so heavily from a past life?

Brown's biographer, Antoinette May, writes that her "suffering has often been intense" and that her "psychic abilities were a burden from which she could never free herself."[100] "The conflicts and challenges that have beset Sylvia are numerous and varied" and "her body, weary of the battle within, was vulnerable to everything. Without understanding the cause, she suffered almost serial illnesses: persistent colds, flu, bronchitis, pneumonia."[101]

What those who want to become psychic do not understand is that psychics bring a great deal of pain, suffering and even tragedy into their lives merely by their choice to become psychic. In 45 years of counseling experience, Dr. Kurt Koch referred to "20,000 terrible cases" and said that when one looks at what occult involvement does in the lives of people, one must warn people against involvement: "Anyone who has had to observe for 45 years the effects of spiritism can only warn people with all the strength at his disposal."[102]

In *The Coming Darkness* (Harvest House, 1993), we spent some 300 pages documenting the danger of psychic practices from the writings of psychics and occultists themselves, Eastern gurus, psychic counselors, and theologians. We documented by example some of the specific consequences including suicide, psychiatric illness and related problems, hereditary coherence and other forms of transference, physical harm, murder, death, disease and torture by the spirits, sexual immorality, spiritual harm and other adverse effects. The further warning of Dr. Koch should be carefully listened to and heeded by everyone even slightly interested in this realm: "Now, if we were to consider the number of cases in which occultism has had a damaging effect on people, our ratio would work out to something in the region of nine out of 10 cases. I could support this fact by means of many thousands of examples."[103]

Further, imagine the consequences of taking psychics' advice and seeking to develop psychic powers in both children and adults. As noted psychologist Robert A. Baker points out, "We should be eternally grateful that if psi forces do exist they are fairly weak and inconsequential. Think what a horrible world it would be if psychokinesis were a fact and could be used at will by anyone. The slightest angry thought could propel a brick, a stone, a chair, a bottle, with deadly force. Cars would be washed from the highways and planes wiped out of the skies by someone's whim. If telepathy were common or universal, privacy would be a thing of the past and the mental effort we would be required to exert to monitor our own as well as other people's thinking processes would leave us little time for ordinary cognitive chores. We would be faced with a world made up of monsters and creatures that would no longer be human. Rather than the boon and blessing that proponents of the paranormal have foreseen, universal access to such full-blown mental powers could destroy civilization as we know it and bring us down more quickly than the most deadly of our nuclear devices. There is much to be said for being as we are."[104] And that is just the point. We are as we are. We are not psychic—except with the "help" of spirits.

And what of the psychics' overall pantheistic philosophy and moral views— aren't these highly consequential to society generally?

Although space does not permit an elaboration, we are convinced that the explosion of interest in the psychic realm, which now fascinates tens of millions of Americans, has done great damage to society and our culture. As we sought to demonstrate elsewhere, ideas such as monism, pantheism, amoralism, and reincarnation have significant social consequences.[105] People not only face the dangers of occult practices associated with these philosophies, but they will also find themselves philosophically or experientially insulated against the gospel message. This will hinder their salvation and also costs society dearly.

Consider as an illustration how the amoral perspective of the occult brings all kinds of personal, familial and cultural consequences. If we look at the problems we face in America today whether it be the culture of self, violent crime, drugs, abortion, divorce, fraud, or whatever, these are all fundamentally *moral* problems. No one can deny that if people lived according to biblical teaching, at least 90 percent of our problems would be solved almost overnight. Given the fact that a culture's quality of life is largely dependent upon its morality, what do you think will be the consequence of our culture adopting the morality found in the world of the psychic? Below we supply representative teachings from various psychics concerning their moral views:

> "One who is truly as loving as Christ would let even the most heinous of murderers continue to commit yet another act [of murder]. . . . 'I was astounded to hear one reading say that killing somebody, in some circumstances, may not be half so sinful as two people agreeing to continue living together for appearances sake when love has gone,' said Ross Peterson. . . . Abortion, as the readings see it, is a minor sin, if indeed it be a sin. . . . The embryo is not a human being,

in the true sense, until the soul enters this vegetative being in the womb."[106]

"Conventional morality, especially Christian morality is a detriment to the soul. . . ."[107]

"You can't stop it if people want to shoot each other up. That's people's way of learning. It's just part of the plan."[108]

"A strong belief in such [concepts of good and evil] is highly detrimental. . . ."[109]

"There is no such thing as evil."[110]

"Obedience [to God] is the greatest sin."[111]

"I don't believe in morality . . . and I am bent on destroying it."[112]

" . . . love the Lord self with every particle of feeling you have"; "Morality involves making choices that are best for you"; "Self-love will nurture and nourish you."[113]

Aren't these the very kinds of beliefs concerning moral values that have so thoroughly undermined the foundations of society and brought such destruction and misery into lives of millions of people? Is giving advice based on a relative morality, a "do your own thing" perspective, going to help or hurt our nation? If tens of millions of people are listening to and following the advice of psychics who listen to spirits— who are really demons—do you think this will help or hurt our nation? Medium and psychic Enid Hoffman writes, "It really is a moot point what guides are, but it does not matter as long as we profit from the guidance they give."[114] Of course, it matters a great deal if the guides are demons. Then their advice, no matter how seemingly good or innocent initially, will have consequences later.

Finally, if all the results of occult philosophy and practice, including its negative impact on morality, spirituality, the family and society generally goes unabated, won't we soon face the likelihood of divine judgment itself?

In conclusion, no one can logically argue that there are no social or national consequences to the burgeoning interests in the psychic realm.

15. Are all psychic experiences negative and can there be neutral or godly psychic experiences?

According to our discussion in this booklet, psychic experiences are neither neutral nor godly nor, in terms of their long-term consequences something positive.

Evangelicals are sometimes divided on the issue of whether or not there is a neutral extrasensory perception. In his cassette tape, "ESP and Parapsychology," the late authority on the cults and the occult, Dr. Walter Martin, provided an illustration of an evangelical Christian in Canada who sensed that her father in Switzerland was greatly ill. She actually saw into the hospital room where he lay, even hearing the conversations of the doctors and nurse. She later confirmed the accuracy of the clairvoyant vision by contacting the medical authorities in Switzerland where her father was in the hospital. Martin classifies this as normal ESP, i.e., apparently not a divine act intended to inspire prayer: "This is normal ESP and if it happens don't get shook up—it has nothing to do with the occult." We agree that a rare ESP event is of little concern and that a person need not worry about it.

The supernatural may occur in the lives of many people. The problem is differentiating the similar or different ways in which God acts toward Christians and non-Christians and how the devil acts toward Christians and non-Christians. For example, there may be a pre-conversion work of God, directly or indirectly through angelic agency that would involve something that could be labeled "psychic." There are also deceptive experiences from the devil and his angels (Matthew. 25:41) that people may interpret as divine.

One cannot always immediately assign a given psychic event to either category until the results of the experience are known.

In some cases "psychic" experiences may result from a kind of linkage between one human spirit and another as in the case of a mother and child who may be connected spiritually/genetically in an unknown manner entirely unrelated to what we today define as psychic. If the Traducean theory of the transmission of the human spirit is correct, in some cases, a mother and child may be "linked" in some unknown fashion in ways that are beyond the biological/psychological. This may even hold true for other family members; the link decreasing in power as proximity to the original source decreases. However, this would not necessitate the conclusion that the human mind or spirit itself is capable of performing miracles. An unknown "linkage" between certain genetically related human spirits does not mean these human spirits can perform supernatural communication outside this linkage, let alone other supernatural events.

Of course, in instances where a mother senses danger to her child, or one family member to another, these could also originate from God or from godly angels rather than an occasional genetically instituted spiritual "linkage." The simple facts that 1) the human spirit is a genuine mystery we know little or nothing about or 2) that man is made in God's image or 3) that "in Him we live and move and have our being" (Acts 17:28) does not require the conclusion that the human spirit itself has supernatural powers. It may have unknown capacities, but that does not necessarily mean it can perform miracles, at least not this side of heaven. A further consideration is that we are ignorant of the exact "spacial" relationship between the material and spiritual worlds; if there is some kind of interpenetration at some level, the fact of accidental crossovers might be possible. If so, then the human mind/spirit could occasionally and instantly interact with or contact the environmental reality of the spiritual world. This would be perceived as a form of ESP but it would not be the same as having an inner nature or "core" structure capable of supernatural powers.

In essence, when examining the case for neutral ESP, we should remember the following: 1) alternate natural explanations may exist for a seeming psychic experience, even though no current explanation is possible; 2) there are things that either God, angels, the devil or demons do that may be falsely interpreted as human ESP; 3) many people have rarely experienced psychic events such as precognition, telepathy, clairvoyance. This does not mean that the potential to become psychic lies within a person apart from any other source. If neutral ESP exists, it would be rare, would not progress to develop psychic abilities, and would give no evidence of spiritual deception or harm at the time of the event or afterward; 4) some psychic experiences may be fading residuals of a family heredity in psychicism and thus only appear neutral; 5) some may result from normal functionings of the human spirit either alone or in conjunction with divine interests; and 6) as the noted astronomer, Carl Sagan, pointed out in a personal anecdote, "some events can certainly initially appear to be psychic or supernatural and yet are actually coincidental." He recalls that at one point he awoke in the dead of night "in a cold sweat, with a *certain* knowledge that a close relative had suddenly died." It turned out the relative had *not* died. But if the relative *had* coincidentally passed on, Sagan recalls, "you would have had a difficult time convincing me that it was merely coincidence."[115]

Regardless, the strongest evidence that man is not latently psychic is the evidence of human history. The *vast* majority of people have *never* developed psychic powers—so how can we possibly say they are latent to humanity?

16. What should you do if you are psychic?

The dangers of psychic involvement are real. If you are currently involved and have not yet experienced the cost, it is only a matter of time. But please know that there is only one way to be delivered from the web of the psychic world—through the power of Jesus Christ. Psychological, psychic, pagan and all other unbiblical approaches can only fail, although they may in some cases temporarily alleviate the symptoms. Solving the problem requires repentance from sin and trust in the biblical Jesus Christ. In order to receive Jesus Christ as your personal Lord and Savior we suggest the following prayer: "Dear God, I now confess my sin of seeking with what you have forbidden and renounce all my psychic involvement and all the spirits associated with it. I ask Jesus Christ to enter my life and to become my Lord and Savior. I believe that on the cross Jesus Christ died for my sin and rose from the dead three days later. I now receive Him into life. I recognize this is a solemn decision that You take very seriously. My commitment to You is that I will follow Christ and I trust You to give me the strength for this. In Jesus' name. Amen."

If you have prayed this prayer we encourage you to write us directly at The John Ankerberg Show. We want to help your growth as a Christian. Next, we suggest that you read a modern, easy to read translation of the Bible such as the New International Version or New American Standard Bible. Start with the New Testament, Psalms and Proverbs and then proceed to the rest of the Scriptures. Also, find a quality church where people honor the Bible and God's Word and Jesus Christ as their personal Lord and Savior. Tell someone of your decision to follow Christ and begin to grow in your new relationship with God by talking to Him daily in prayer.

NOTES

1. An editor at Time-Life books told us that their lengthy 32 volume book series on the psychic realm, *Mysteries of the Unknown*, has been the best-selling series in their entire history, outselling all other series. That such a lengthy series on the psychic world should outsell other popular series about dieting, woodworking, war, cooking, gardening, fitness, health and nutrition, parenting, healthy home cooking, understanding computers, creative photography, home repair and improvement, and the Old West, is hardly insignificant.

2. The material in this paragraph comes from Mensah Dean, "Future Looking Bright for 'Psychic' Networks," *Washington Times*, May 9, 1996, (photocopy of one page article, page number not Xeroxed); the transcript of Janet Parshall's America—"Psychics" for July 19, 1996, p. 6, containing an interview with Linda Georgian and John Weldon.

3. Transcript.

4. Ibid., pp. 6-7, cf., David S. Fondiller, "And Who's To Say They're Wrong?", *Forbes*, June 17, 1996.

5. Ibid., pp. 6-7.

6. Dean, op. cit., ibid.

7. *Oxford American Dictionary* (NY: Avon, 1982), p. 723.

8. *Macmillan Dictionary for Students* (NY: Macmillan, 1984), p. 807.

9. Litany Burns, *Develop Your Psychic Abilities* (NY: Pocketbooks, 1987), pp. i, 44-45.

10. Loretta R. Washburn, *Mind Travelers: Portraits of Famous Psychics and Healers of Today* (Norfolk, VA: Hampton Roads Publishing, 1994), p. 16.

11. C. Eugene Emery, Jr., "Telephone Psychics: Friends or Phonies?" *Skeptical Inquirer*, September/October 1995, p. 14.

12. Health Tech, Inc., *The Hottest Products and Information Guide: Secrets to Making Money* (Health Tech, Inc., 1996, npp), p. 30.

13. Emery, Jr., p. 16.

14. In the words of C. Eugene Emery, Jr., p. 16.

15. Washburn, p. 25.

16. Emery, Jr., p. 17.

17. Cited in his book review of *The Cosmic Self: A Penetrating Look at Today's New Age Movements* in *Christianity Today*, photocopy of article undated. The book review section was titled "The Demons Next Door," and it included reviews of Carl Rashke's *Painted Black* (on Satanism) and *The Cosmic Self*, pp. 56-57.

18. George H. Gallup, Jr. and Frank Newport, "Belief in Paranormal Phenomena Among Adult Americans," *The Skeptical Inquirer*, Winter 1991, pp. 137-46, cf., Andrew Greeley, "Mysticism Goes Mainstream," *American Health*, January/February, 1987.

19. Jon Klimo, *Channeling: Investigations on Receiving Information from Paranormal Sources* (Los Angeles: Jeremy P. Tarcher, Inc., 1987), p. 3.

20. Cited in *National and International Religion Report*, July 4, 1988, p. 1.

21. Enid Hoffman, *Develop Your Psychic Skills* (Rochester, MA: Para Research, Inc., 1981), p. 5.

22. Ibid., p. 10.

23. For example Helen Schuchman's *A Course in Miracles*, *The Urantia Book* and other volumes, cf., John Ankerberg, John Weldon, *Encyclopedia of New Age Beliefs* (Eugene, OR: Harvest House, 1996), pp. 101-106, for more examples.

24. "Psi Trek: The Real 'X Files,'" on the *Discovery Channel*, September 2, 1996, 9 P.M.

25. Ibid.

26. The above material is take from the TV program "Sightings," May 30, 1996. See the more comprehensive evaluation by Ray Hyman, "Evaluation

of the Military's 20-year Program on Psychic Spying," *Skeptical Inquirer*, March/April 1996 and "Psi Trek: The Real 'X Files.'" Science writer Jim Schnabel was a key researcher for the TV program on the Discovery Channel, "Psi Trek: The Real 'X Files,'" which aired September 2, 1996. He is currently working on a book on the subject to be published in 1997 which will detail the government's involvement with psychics, channelers and other occultists.

27. See our *The Facts on Angels* for an evaluation of the modern angel phenomenon.

28. Notes taken from a TV special, the time and date of which were not recorded, but see footnote 26, especially the forthcoming book by Schnabel.

29. Donald T. Regan, *For the Record: From Wall Street to Washington* (NY: Harcourt Brace Jovanovich, 1988), pp. xiv, 3-4, 68-74, 300-01.

30. See "Hillary's Other Side," *Newsweek*, July 1, 1996, pp. 26-29.

31. Jean Houston, *The Possible Human: A Course in Extending Your Physical, Mental, and Creative Abilities* (Los Angeles: J. P. Tarcher, 1982), pp. 177-80.

32. Nandor Fodor, *An Encyclopedia of Psychic Science* (Secaucus, NJ: Citadel, 1974), p. 310.

33. Hans Holzer, *The Directory of the Occult* (Chicago: Henry Regnery, 1974), p. 197.

34. Hope Andrews, *Do Psychics Really Know?* (Chesapeake, VA: Creations of Hope, 1994), pp. 111, 173-74, but see footnote 26, especially the forthcoming book by Schnabel.

35. Washburn, respectively, pp. 21, 25, 27, 31, 35, 43, 44, 51, 55, 57, 61, 63, 67, 71, 77, 81, 85, 93, 95, 99, 105, 115, 119.

36. Hans Holzer, *The Directory of Psychics* (Chicago, IL: Contemporary Books, 1995), p. 182, cf., pp. vi-viii, 1, 7, 27-29, 35, 43-44, 47, 73, 89, 182.

37. Ibid., p. vii.

38. Ibid., pp. 104-11.

39. Ibid., pp. 108-09.

40. Naomi A. Hintze and J. Gaither Pratt, *The Psychic Realm: What Can You Believe?* (NY: Random House, 1975), pp. 117-254.

41. Douglas and Barbara Dillon, *An Explosion of Being: An American Family's Journey Into the Psychic* (West Nyack, NY: Parker Publishing, 1984).

42. Leslie A. Shepard, (ed.), *Encyclopedia of Occultism and Parapsychology*, (Detroit, MI: Gale Research Co., 2 Vols., 1979, rev.), Vol. 2, p. 692, emphasis added.

43. Louisa Rhine, *PSI—What Is It—An Introduction to Parapsychology* (New York: Harper and Row, 1975), p. 2.

44. David Hammond, "Psychic Evolution and You," *Psychic Magazine*, April, 1976, p. 21.

45. Howard M. Zimmermann, "Introduction," in Benjamin B. Wolman, (ed.), *Handbook of Parapsychology* (New York: Van Nostrand Reinhold Co., 1977), p. XVII, passim.

46. See e.g., Clifford Wilson and John Weldon, *Psychic Forces and Occult Shock* (Chattanooga, TN: Global, 1987), chapters 22-25.

47. Bejamin B. Wolman, (ed.), *Handbook of Parapsychology* (NY: Van Nostrand Reinhold Co., 1977), pp. 5, 27-29; Gardner Murphy, *The Challenge Of Psychical Research* (New York: Harper-Colophon Books, 1970), p. 185.

48. Wilson and Weldon, pp. 343-49, see the discussion in Alfred Douglas', *Extra-Sensory Powers: A Century of Psychical Research* (Woodstock, NY: Overlook Press, 1977), especially chapter 4, "Early Investigations"; also Alan Gauld, *The Founders Of Psychical Research* (New York: Shocken Books, 1968).

49. D. Scott Rogo, *Parapsychology: A Century of Inquiry* (New York: Dell, 1975), p. 44.

50. Fodor, *Encyclopedia of Psychic Science*, p. 316, emphasis added.

51. Colin Wilson, *Dark Dimensions: A Celebration of the Occult* (NY: Everest House, 1977), p. 10.

52. John Ankerberg, John Weldon, *Astrology: Do the Heavens Rule Our Destiny?* (Eugene, OR: Harvest House, 1990).

53. Ankerberg, Weldon, *Encyclopedia of New Age Beliefs*, p. 63.

54. *Skeptical Inquirer*, January/February 1996, p. 5.

55. Transcript, p. 10.

56. *Skeptical Inquirer*, March/April. 1996, p. 17.

57. Jeane Dixon, *The Call to Glory: Jeane Dixon Speaks of Jesus* (NY: Bantam, 1973 edition), p. 154.

58. Ibid., p. 166-168.

59. Reverend Beverly Burdick-Carey, *Ascended Masters Speak to Us Today* (Chesapeake, VA: Creations of Hope, n.d.), respectively pp. 9, 13-14, 19-20.

60. Ambrose A. Worrall, Olga N. Worrall, *Explore Your Psychic World* (NY: Harper & Row, 1970), pp. 1-4.

61. This world view is readily seen in the literature e.g., *Psychics* magazine (now *New Realities*) Vol. 1, no. 1 to the present.

62. John Ankerberg, John Weldon, *The Coming Darkness* (Eugene: OR: Harvest House, 1993), pp. 207-215.

63. Fodor, p. 233.

64. Kurt Koch, *Christian Counseling and Occultism* (Grand Rapids, MI: Kregel, 1978), pp. 117-18.

65. The editors of *Psychic Psychics: Indepth Interviews* (NY: Harper & Row, 1972), pp. 16, 35, 47, 68, 79, 104, 113.

66. Sylvia Brown and Antoinette May, *Adventures of a Psychic* (NY: Signet, 1991), p. 1.

67. Holzer, *The Directory of Psychics*, p. 135.

68. Ankerberg, Weldon, *Encyclopedia of New Age Beliefs*, pp. 246, 387-89, cf., Index categories "Possession," "Psychic Abilities," and "Psychic Development."

69. Swami Anand Yarti Comp., *The Sound of Running Water: A Photo-Biography of Bhagwan Shree Rajaneesh and His Work 1974-1978* (Poona, India: Rajaneesh Foundation, 1980), p. 68.

70. Rudi (Swami Rudrananda), *Spiritual Cannibalism* (Woodstock, NY: Overlook, 1978), p. 20.

71. See the chapter on Dowsing in our *Encyclopedia of New Age Beliefs*.

72. Kurt Koch, *Demonology Past and Present* (Grand Rapids, MI: Kregel, 1971), p. 62.

73. Melita Denning and Osborne Phillips, *The Development of Psychic Powers* (St. Paul, MN: Llewellyn Publications, 1985), pp. 192-93.

74. Fodor, p. 238.

75. See our critique in *Cult Watch: What You Need to Know About Spiritual Deception* (Eugene, OR: Harvest House, 1991), pp. 277-281.

76. John Beloff, "Historical Overview," in Wolman (ed.), p. 21.

77. Danny Korem, "Waging War Against Deception," *Christianity Today*, April 18, 1986, p. 32.

78. Michael Harner, *The Way Of The Shaman* (New York: Bantam, 1986), p. 54.

79. Mircea Eliade, Shamanism: *Archaic Techniques Of Ecstasy Princeton* (NJ: Bollingen/Princeton University Press, 1974), passim; see the comments by Dr. Robert S. Ellwood, Jr. in *Religious and Spiritual Groups In Modern America* (Englewood Clifts, NJ: Prentice-Hall, 1973), "The [Modern] Cult Phenomena Could Almost Be Called A Modern Resurgence Of Shamanism," p. 10; also Tal Brooke, *Riders of the Cosmic Circuit: Rajaneesh, Sai Baba, Muktananda . . . God's of the New Age* (Batavia: IL, Lyon, 1986), cf. Mircea Eliade, *From Primitives to Zen: A Thematic Source Book of the History Of Religions* (New York: Harper and Row, 1977).

80. Sayed Idries Shah, *Oriental Magic* (New York: E. P. Dutton, 1973), p. 123.

81. Louis Jacolliot, *Occult Science in India and Among The Ancients*, (New Hyde Park, NY: University Books, 1971), p. 201.

82. Ibid., p. 204.

83. Jess Stearn, *Adventures Into The Psychic* (New York, Signet, 1982), p. 163.

84. Doreen Irvine, *Freed From Witchcraft* (Nashville, TN: Thomas Nelson, 1973), p. 96.

85. Ibid., p. 123.

86. Ibid., p. 7.

87. David Conway, *Magic: An Occult Primer* (NY: Bantam, 1973), p. 19.

88. Eileen J. Garrett, *Many Voices: The Autobiography of a Medium* (NY: Dell, 1969), pp. 86-88.

89. Charles Panati, *Supersenses* (Garden City, NY: Anchor/Doubleday, 1976), p. 102.

90. George W. Meek, "The Healers in Brazil, England, U.S.A., and U.S.S.R.," in George W. Meek (ed.), *Healers And The Healing Process: A Report on Ten Years of Research by Fourteen World Famous Investigators* (Wheaton, IL: Theosophical/Quest, 1977), p. 32.

91. Jeanne Pontius Rindge, "Perspective—An Overview Of Paranormal Healing," in Meek (ed.), p. 17.

92. Hans Naegeli-Osjord, "Psychiatric and Psychological Considerations," in Meek (ed.), p. 80.

93. The editors of *Psychic Psychics: Indepth Interviews*, p. 89.

94. In Wilson, *The Psychic Detectives: The Story of Psychometry and Paranormal Crime Detection* (San Francisco: Mercury House, 1985), p. 132.

95. Ibid., pp. 138-39.

96. Ankerberg, Weldon, *Encyclopedia of New Age Beliefs.* e.g., pp. 14-16, 21, 85-86, 116.

97. Burns, p. 149.

98. Ibid., p. 166, 225.

99. Brown and May, pp. 1-2.

100. Ibid., pp. 22, 25.

101. Ibid,. pp. 37, 43.

102. Kurt Koch, *Occult ABC* (West Germany: Literature Mission Aglasterhausen, Inc., 1980), pp. 238, 282; cf., his *Occult Bondage and Deliverance* (Grand Rapids, MI: Kregel, 1970), p. 31.

103. Koch, *Occult Bondage and Deliverance*, p. 30.

104. Robert A. Baker, *They Call It Hypnosis* (Buffalo, NY: Promethius, 1990), p. 225.

105. E.g., *The Coming Darkness*, Chs. 2, 13, App. C, cf., our forthcoming critique of reincarnation.

106. Allen Spraggett, *Ross Peterson: The New Edgar Cayce* (Garden City, NY: Doubleday, 1977), pp. 141-42, 148-50.

107. Personal conversation.

108. Jenny Randles, *Beyond Explanation? The Paranormal Experiences of Famous People* (Manchester, NH: Salem House, 1985), p. 148. The statement is by a spirit entity.

109. Jane Roberts, *Seth Speaks* (Prentice Hall, 1972), p. 191

110. J. Z. Knight in Douglas Mahr's *Ramtha, Voyage to the New World* (NY: Valentine, 1987), p. 60.

111. Bhagwan Shree Rajaneesh, *The Rajaneesh Bible*, Vol. 1, (Rajneeshpuram, OR: Rajaneesh Foundation International, 1985), p. 368.

112. Bhagwan Shree Rajaneesh, "I Am The Messiah, Here And Now," *Sannyas*, No. 5, 1978, p. 34.

113. John Randolph Price, *The Angels Within Us: A Spiritual Guide to the Twenty-two Angels that Govern Our Lives* (NY: Fawcett, 1993), p. 63; Terry Lynn Taylor, Mary Beth Crain, *Angel Wisdom: 365 Meditations and Insights from the Heavens* (NY: HarperCollins, 1994) for September 8; Terry Lynn Taylor, *Creating with the Angels: An Angel-Guided Journey into Creativity* (Tiburon, CA: H. J. Kramer, 1993), p. 152.

114. Hoffman, p. 152.

115. Carl Sagan in *Skeptical Inquirer*, Spring 1986, p. 221.